LOVE RESPELT

LOVE RESPELT

ROBERT GRAVES

1966

DOUBLEDAY & COMPANY, INC.

GARDEN CITY, NEW YORK

FOREWORD

LOVE RESPELT was first published on July 24th, 1965, my seventieth birthday, by Messrs. Cassell & Co., in London in a limited edition of 250 copies, with designs by Aemilia Lara-çuen. The poems were photographed from my manuscript.

This edition contains the poems printed in the last section of my COLLECTED POEMS 1965, also by Messrs. Cassell. I have been asked to supply a foreword, but find nothing of importance to say, because poems should explain themselves, unless perhaps that Batxóca (with the x pronounced as *ch*) is a Majorcan word meaning "bean-like" or "over-imaginative" as beans run crazily up their poles. So I am using the pages allotted me for seven more poems that form part of the sequence, which was written in England, Spain, New York and Mexico. Some belong to the beginning, some to the end.

R.G.

DEYÁ
MALLORCA
SPAIN

CONTENTS

XVIII

XVIII

THE RED SHOWER

Live sparks rain from the central anvil
  In a red shower. Let all beware
Who read the event as history, frowning at
  What they may find of madness there:
  Felicity endangering despair.

ABOVE THE EDGE OF DOOM

Bats at play taunt us with 'guess how many',
And music sounds far off, tempered by sea.
Above the edge of doom sits woman
Communing with herself. 'Dear love,' says she,
As it were apostrophizing cat or dog,
'Sometimes by a delicate glance and gesture
You almost seem to understand me,
Poor honest creature of the blue eyes,
Having crept closer to my sealed bosom
With your more desperate faith in womankind
Than any other since I first flowered.

It may be best you cannot read my mind.'

WILD CYCLAMEN

'What can I do for you?' she asked gently.
I reached for pen and paper: 'Draw me flowers!'

She pursed her lips—O the smooth brown forehead,
The smooth lids drooped, intent on their task—
And drew me wild Majorcan cyclamen
(Not yet in season) extravagantly petalled,
Then laughed and tossed me back the picture.

'It is nothing,' she said; yet that cyclamen odour
Hung heavy in the room for a long while;
And when she was gone, I caught myself smiling
In her own crooked way, trying to make my eyes
Sparkle like hers, though ineffectually,
Till I fell asleep; for this was my sick-bed
And her visits brief, by order.

GIFT OF SIGHT

I had long known the diverse tastes of the wood,
Each leaf, each bark, rank earth from every hollow;
Knew the smells of bird's breath and of bat's wing;
Yet sight I lacked: until you stole upon me,
Touching my eyelids with light finger-tips.
The trees blazed out, their colours whirled together,
Nor ever before had I been aware of sky.

BATXÓCA

Firm-lipped, high-bosomed, slender Queen of Beanstalk
                                                    Land,
Who are more to me than any woman upon this earth
Though you live from hand to mouth, keeping no certain
                                                    hours,
Disguising your wisdom with unpracticality
And your elusiveness with hugs for all and sundry,
Flaunting green, yellow and scarlet, suddenly disappearing
In a whirlwind rage and flurry of skirts, always alone
Until found, days later, asleep on a couch of broom
And incommunicable until you have breakfasted—
By what outrageous freak of dissimilarity
Were you forced, noble Batxóca, to fall so deep in love
With me as to demand marriage, despite your warning
That you and I must on no account be seen together—
A Beanstalk Queen, no less, paired with a regular man!

Did you wistfully, perhaps, expect me to say 'no'?

THE SNAP-COMB WILDERNESS

Magic is tangled in a woman's hair
For the enlightenment of male pride.
To slide a comb uxoriously
Through an even swell of tresses undisturbed
By their cascade from an exact parting
Could never hearten or enlighten me—
Not though her eyes were bluer than blue sea.
Magic rules an irreducible jungle
Dark as eclipse and scented with despair,
A stubborn snap-comb wilderness of hair,
Each strand a singular, wild, curling tree.

A SHIFT OF SCENE

To lie far off, in bed with a foul cough,
And a view of elms and roofs and six panes' worth
Of clear sky; here to watch, all the day long,
For a dove, or a black cat, or a puff of smoke
To cause a shift of scene—how could it do so?—
Or to take a pen and write—what else is there
To write but: 'I am not dead, not quite, as yet
Though I lie far off, in bed with a foul cough
And a view of elms and roofs and six panes' worth
Of clear sky'? Tell me, love, are you sick too
And plagued like me with a great hole in the mind
Where all those towers we built, and not on sand,
Have been sucked in and lost; so that it seems
No dove, and no black cat, nor puff of smoke
Can cause a shift of scene and fetch us back
To where we lie as one, in the same bed?

CHANGE

'This year she has changed greatly'—meaning you—
My sanguine friends agree,
And hope thereby to reassure me.

No, child, you never change; neither do I.
Indeed all our lives long
We are still fated to do wrong,

Too fast caught by care of humankind,
Easily vexed and grieved,
Foolishly flattered and deceived;

And yet each knows that the changeless other
Must love and pardon still,
Be the new error what it will:

Assured by that same glint of deathlessness
Which neither can surprise
In any other pair of eyes.

A COURT OF LOVE

Were you to break the vow we swore together,
The vow, I said, would break you utterly:
Despite your pleas of duty elsewhere owed,
You could no longer laugh, work, heal, do magic,
Nor in the mirror face your own eyes.

They have summoned me before their Court of Love
And warned me I must sign for your release
Pledging my word never again to draft
A similar pact, as one who has presumed
Lasting felicity still unknown in time.
What should I do? Forswear myself for you?
No man in love, plagued by his own scruples
Will ever, voluntarily, concede
That women have a spirit above vows.

BLACK

Black drinks the sun and draws all colours to it.
I am bleached white, my truant love. Come back,
And stain me with intensity of black.

BETWEEN HYSSOP AND AXE

To know our destiny is to know the horror
Of separation, dawn oppressed by night:
Is, between hyssop and axe, boldly to prove
That gifted, each, with singular need for freedom
And haunted, both, by spectres of reproach,
We may yet house together without succumbing
To the low fever of domesticity
Or to the lunatic spin of aimless flight.

SON ALTESSE

Alone, you are no more than many another
Gay-hearted, greedy, passionate noblewoman;
And I, alone, no more than a slow-witted
Passionate, credulous knight, though skilled in fight.

Then if I hail you as my Blessed Virgin
This is no flattery, nor does it endow you
With private magics which, when I am gone,
May flatter rogues or drunken renegades.

Name me your single, proud, whole-hearted champion
Whose feats no man alive will overpass;
But they must reverence you as I do; only
Conjoined in fame can we grow legendary.

Should I ride home, vainglorious after battle,
With droves of prisoners and huge heaps of spoil,
Make me dismount a half-mile from your door;
To walk barefoot in dust, as a knight must.

Yet never greet me carelessly or idly,
Nor use the teasing manners learned at Court,
Lest I be ambushed in a treacherous pass—
And you pent up in shame's black nunnery.

GOLD AND MALACHITE

After the hour of illumination, when the tottering mind
Has been by force delivered from its incubus of despair,
When all the painted, papier mâché, Mexican faces
Of demons grinning at you from hell's vaulted roof
Fade and become angelic monitors of wisdom—
Slowly the brisk intelligence wakes, to mutter questions
Of when, where, how; and which should be the first step
                                        forward. . . .

Now is the crucial moment you were forewarned against.
Stop your ears with your fingers, guard unequivocal silence
Lest you discuss wisdom in the language of unwisdom;
Roam instead through the heaped treasury of your heart:
You will find her, from whom you have been so long
                                        estranged,
Chin to knees, brooding apart on gold and malachite.
But beware again: even a shy embrace would be too
                                        explicit—
Let her learn by your gait alone that you are free at last.

AMBIENCE

The nymph of the forest, only in whose honour
These birds perform, provides an ambience
But never leads the chorus: even at dawn
When we awake to whistle, flute and pipe,
Astonished they can so extemporize
Their own parts, as it were haphazard
Each in his own time, yet avoid discordance
Or domineering, however virtuose
Or long sustained each voluntary of love.
The rare silences, too, appear like sound
Rather than pause for breath or meditation. . . .
Nor is the same piece ever given twice.

THE VOW

No vow once sworn may ever be annulled
Except by a higher law of love or mercy—
Search your heart well: is there a lie hidden
Deep in its convolutions of resolve?

For whom do you live? Can it be yourself?
For whom then? Not for this unlovely world,
Not for the rotting waters of mischance,
Nor for the tall, eventual catafalque.

You live for her who alone loves you,
Whose royal prerogative can be denied
By none observant of the awakening gasps
That greet her progress down whatever hall.

Your vow is to truth, not practicality;
To honour, not to the dead world's esteem;
To a bed of rock, not to a swan's-down pillow;
To the tears you kiss away from her black eyes.

They lament an uninstructible world of men
Who dare not listen or watch, but challenge proof
That a leap of a thousand miles is nothing
And to walk invisibly needs no artifice.

THE FROG AND THE GOLDEN BALL

She let her golden ball fall down the well
   And begged a cold frog to retrieve it;
For which she kissed his ugly, gaping mouth—
   Indeed, he could scarce believe it.

And seeing him transformed to his princely shape,
   Who had been by hags enchanted,
She knew she could never love another man
   Nor by any fate be daunted.

But what would her royal father and mother say?
   They had promised her in marriage
To a cousin whose wide kingdom marched with theirs,
   Who rode in a jewelled carriage.

'Our plight, dear heart, would appear past human hope
   To all except you and me: to all
Who have never swum as a frog in a dark well
   Or have lost a golden ball.'

'What then shall we do now?' she asked her lover.
   He kissed her again, and said:
'Is magic of love less powerful at your Court
   Than at this green well-head?'

THOSE WHO CAME SHORT

Those who came short of love for me or you,
Where are they now? Ill-starred and bitter-mouthed,
Cursing us for their own contrariness,
Each having fallen in turn, head over heels,
From that illusive heaven at which they flew.

Are we then poison of love-perfection
To all but our own kind? Should we beware
Of handling such intemperate shaggy creatures
As leap on us like dogs to be cosseted
And, after, claim full rights of jealousy?

At once too simple and too various
Except for ourselves, should we awhile conceal
Our studies from the world, in cool forbearance
Watching each night for another dawn to break
And the last guest to straggle home?

WHOLE LOVE

Every choice is always the wrong choice,
Every vote cast is always cast away—
How can truth hover between alternatives?

Then love me more than dearly, love me wholly,
Love me with no weighing of circumstance,
As I am pledged in honour to love you:

With no weakness, with no speculation
On what might happen should you and I prove less
Than bringers-to-be of our own certainty.
Neither was born by hazard: each foreknew
The extreme possession we are grown into.

THIS HOLY MONTH

The demon who throughout our late estrangement
Followed with malice in my footsteps, often
Making as if to stumble, so that I stumbled
And gashed my head against a live rock;
Who tore my palms on butcher's broom and thorn,
Flung me at midnight into filthy ditches
And multiplied the horrors of this house
When back I limped again to a hard bed;
Who simultaneously plagued you too
With sleeplessness, dismay and darkness,
Paralysed your hands, denied you air—
We both know well he was the same demon,
Arch-enemy of rule and calculation,
Who lives for our love, being created from it,
Astonishes us with blossom, silvers the hills
With more than moonlight, summons bees in swarms
From the Lion's mouth to fill our hives with honey,
Turns flesh into fire, and eyes into deep lakes;
And so may do once more, this holy month.

THE IMPOSSIBLE

Dear love, since the impossible proves
  Our sole recourse from this distress,
Claim it: the ebony ritual-mask of no
  Cannot outstare a living yes.

Claim it without despond or hate
  Or greed; but in your gentler tone
Say: 'This is ours, the impossible,' and silence
  Will give consent it is ours alone.

The impossible has wild-cat claws
  Which you would rather meet and die
Than commit love to time's curative venom
  And break our oath; for so would I.

THE FETTER

Concerned, against our wish, with a sick world,
Self-neglectful, tuned to knock or summons,
We make amends for follies not our own.

We have taken love through a thousand deaths;
Should either try to slip our iron fetter,
It bites yet deeper into neck and arm.

As for that act of supererogation,
The kiss in which we secretly concur,
Let laughter mitigate its quiet excess.

Could we only be a simple, bickering pair
In the tied cottage of a small estate,
With no tasks laid on us except to dig,
Hoe, fatten geese and scrape the quarter's rent,
How admirable our close interdependence;
Our insecurity how fortunate!

IRON PALACE

We stood together, side by side, rooted
At the iron heart of circumambient hills,
Parents to a new age, weeping in awe
That the lot had fallen, of all mankind, on us
Now sealed as love's exemplars.

We could not prevaricate or argue,
Citing involvement in some alien scene,
Nor plead unworthiness: none else would venture
To live detached from force of circumstance
As history neared its ending.

We told no one. These were not strange dreams
Recalled at breakfast with a yawning smile,
Nor tales for children, on the verge of sleep,
Who ask no questions. Our predicament
Remained a silent burden.

We had no token or proof, and needed none
Of what we learned that day; but laughed softly
Watching our hands engage, in co-awareness
That these red hills warned us, on pain of death,
Never to disengage them.

Woman, wild and hard as the truth may be,
Nothing can circumvent it. We stand coupled
With chains, who otherwise might live apart
Conveniently paired, each with another,
And slide securely graveward.

24

TRUE JOY

Whoever has drowned and awhile entered
The adamantine gates of afterwards,
Stands privileged to reject heavenly joy
(Though without disrespect for God's archangels)
With 'never again'—no moon, no herbs, no sea,
No singular love of women.

True joy, believe us, is to groan and wake
From the hallelujah choir on Fiddler's Green,
With lungs now emptied of salt water,
With gradual heat returning to clammed veins
In the first flicker of reanimation,
Repossession of now, awareness
Of her live hands and lips, her playful voice,
Her smooth and wingless shoulders.

TOMORROW'S ENVY OF TODAY

Historians may scorn the close engagement
Of Moon with Lion that we have witnessed
Here in this lair, here in this numinous grove,
May write me down as imbecile, or presume
A clot of madness festering in your heart—
Such is tomorrow's envy of today.

Today we are how we are, and how we see:
Alive, elate, untrimmed, without hazard
Of supersession: flowers that never fade
Leaves that never shrivel, truth persistent
Not as a prophecy of bliss to fall
A thousand generations hence on lovers
More fortunately circumstanced than we,
But as a golden interlock of power
Looped about every bush and branching tree.

THE HIDDEN GARDEN

Nor can ambition make this garden theirs,
Any more than birds can fly through a window pane.
When they hint at passwords, keys and private stairs,
We are tempted often to open the front gate,
Which has no lock, and haul them bodily in,
Abashed that there they wait, disconsolate.

And yet such pity would be worse than pride:
Should we admit as love their vain self-pity,
The gate must vanish and we be left outside.

THE WEDDING

When down I went to the rust-red quarry
I was informed, by birds, of your resolve
To live with me for ever and a day—
The day being always new and antecedent.
What could we ask of Nature? Nothing more
Than to outdo herself in our behalf.

Blossoms of caper, though they smell sweet,
Have never sailed the air like butterflies
Circling in innocent dance around each other
Over the cliff and out across the bay;
Nor has broom-blossom scorched a man's finger
With golden fire, kindled by sun.

Come, maids of honour and pages chosen
To attend this wedding, charged to perform
Incomparable feats—dance, caper-blossom!
Scorch, blossom of broom, our married fingers—
Though crowds of almost-men and almost-women
Howl for their lost immediacy.

EVERYWHERE IS HERE

By this exchange of eyes, this encirclement
You of me, I of you, together we baffle
Logic no doubt, but never understanding;
And laugh instead of choking back the tears
When we say goodbye.
                                    Fog gathers thick about us
Yet a single careless pair of leaves, one green, one gold,
Whirl round and round each other skippingly
As though blown by a wind; pause and subside
In a double star, the gold above the green.

Everywhere is here, once we have shattered
The iron-bound laws of contiguity,
Blazoning love as an eagle with four wings
(Their complementary tinctures counterchanged)
That scorns to roost in any terrene crag.

WHAT WILL BE, IS

Manifest reason glared at you and me
Thus ringed with love. Entire togetherness
Became for us the sole redress.

Together in heart, but our over-eager bodies
Distrained upon for debt, we shifted ground;
Which brought mistiming. Each cried out in turn,
And with a complementary delusion:
'I am free; but you? Are you still bound?'

In blood the debts were paid. Hereafter
We make no truce for manifest reason
From this side of the broad and fateful stream
Where wisdom rules from her dark cave of dream
And time is corrigible by laughter.

Moon and Sun are one. Granted, they ride
Paths unconformable to the calendar,
And seldom does a New Moon coincide
With a New Year; yet we agree:
'What will be, is'—rejoicing at a day
Of dolphins jostling in the blue bay,
Eagles in air, and flame on every tree.

SONG: THE FAR SIDE OF YOUR MOON

The far side of your moon is black,
  And glorious grows the vine;
Ask anything of me you lack,
  But only what is mine.

Yours is the great wheel of the sun,
  And yours the unclouded sky;
Then take my stars, take every one,
  But wear them openly.

Walking in splendour through the plain
  For all the world to see,
Since none alive shall view again
  The match of you and me.

DELIVERANCE

Lying disembodied under the trees
(Their slender trunks converged above us
Like rays of a five-fold star) we heard
A sudden whinnying from the dark hill.

Our implacable demon, foaled by love,
Never knew rein or saddle; though he drank
From a stream winding by, his blue pastures
Ranged far out beyond the stellar mill.

He had seared us two so close together
That death itself might not disjoin us;
It was impossible you could love me less,
It was impossible I could love you more.

We were no calculating lovers
But gasped in awe at our deliverance
From a too familiar prison,
And vainly puzzled how it was that now
We should never need to build another,
As each, time after time, had done before.

CONJUNCTION

What happens afterwards, none need enquire:
They are poised there in conjunction, beyond time,
At an oak-tree top level with Paradise:
Its leafy tester unshaken where they stand
Palm to palm, mouth to mouth, beyond desire,
Perpetuating lark song, perfume, colour,
And the tremulous gasp of watchful winds,

Past all unbelief, we know them held
By peace and light and irrefragable love—
Twin paragons, our final selves, resistant
To the dull pull of earth dappled with shade:
Myself the forester, never known to abandon
His vigilant coursing of the greenwood's floor,
And you, dryad of dryads, never before
Yielding her whole heart to the enemy, man.

NOTHING NOW ASTONISHES

A month of vigilance draws to its close
With silence of snow and the Northern lights
In longed-for wordlessness.

This rainbow spanning our two worlds
Becomes more than a bridge between them:
They fade into geography.

Variegated with the seven colours
We twist them into skeins for hide and seek
In a lovers' labyrinth.

Can I be astonished at male trembling
Of sea-horizons as you lean towards them?
Nothing now astonishes.

You change, from a running drop of pure gold
On a silver salver, to the white doe
In nut-groves harbouring.

Let me be changed now to an eight-petalled
Scarlet anemone that will never strain
For the circling butterfly.

Rest, my loud heart. Your too exultant flight
Had raised the wing-beat to a roar
Drowning seraphic whispers.

POSTSCRIPT

I'd die for you, or you for me,
So furious is our jealousy—
And if you doubt this to be true
Kill me outright, lest I kill you.

THE GORGE

Yonder beyond all hope of access
Begins your queendom; here is my frontier.
Between us two howl ghosts of the long dead;
But the bridge that I cross, concealed from view
Even in sunlight (and the gorge bottomless),
Swings and echoes under my strong tread
Because I have need of you.

ARREARS OF MOONLIGHT

My heart lies wrapped in red under your pillow,
My body wanders banished among the stars,
On one terrestrial pretext or another
You still withhold the extravagant arrears
Of moonlight that you owe us,
Though the owl whoops from a far olive branch
His brief, monotonous, nightlong reminder.

THE TANGLED THREAD

Desire, first, by a natural miracle
United bodies, united hearts, blazed beauty;
Transcended bodies, transcended hearts.

Two souls, now unalterably one
In whole love always and for ever,
Soar out of twilight, through upper air,
Let fall their sensuous burden.

Is it kind, though, is it honest even,
To consort with none but spirits—
Leaving true-wedded hearts like ours
In enforced night-long separation
Each to its random bodily inclination,
The thread of miracle tangled, not snapped.

LURE OF MURDER

A round moon suffocates the neighbouring stars
With greener light than sun through vine-leaves.
Tamed by her ecstasy of solitude
I crouch among rocks, scanning the gulf, agape,
Whetting a knife on my horny sole.

Alas for the lure of murder, dear my love:
Could its employment purge two moon-vexed hearts
Of jealousy more formidable than death,
Then each would stab, stab, stab, at secret parts
Of the other's beloved body where unknown
Zones of desire imperil full possession.

But never can mortal dagger serve to geld
This glory of ours, this loving beyond reason—
Death holds no remedy or alternative:
We are singled out to endure his lasting grudge
On the tall battlements of nightfall.

FORTUNATE CHILD

6 For fear strangers might intrude upon us
You and I played at being strangers,
But lent our act such verisimilitude
That when at last, by hazard, we met alone
In a secret glen where the badger earths
We had drawn away from love: did not prepare
For melting of eyes into hearts of flowers,
For a sun-aureoled enhancement of hair,
For over-riding of death on an eagle's back—
Yet so it was: sky shuddered apart before us
Until, from a cleft of more than light, we both
Overheard the laugh of a fortunate child
Swung from those eagle talons in a gold cloth.

LOVING TRUE, FLYING BLIND

How often have I said before
That no soft 'if', no 'either-or',
Can keep my obdurate male mind
From loving true and flying blind?

Which though deranged beyond all cure
Of temporal reason, knows for sure
That timeless magic first began
When woman bared her soul to man.

Be bird, be blossom, comet, star,
Be paradisal gates ajar,
But still, as woman, cleave you must
To who alone endures your trust.

DANCING FLAME

Pass now in metaphor beyond birds,
Their seasonal nesting and migration,
Their airy frolics, their repetitive cries,
Beyond all creatures but our own selves:
Eternal genii of dancing flame
Armed with the irreproachable secret
Of love, which is: never to turn back.